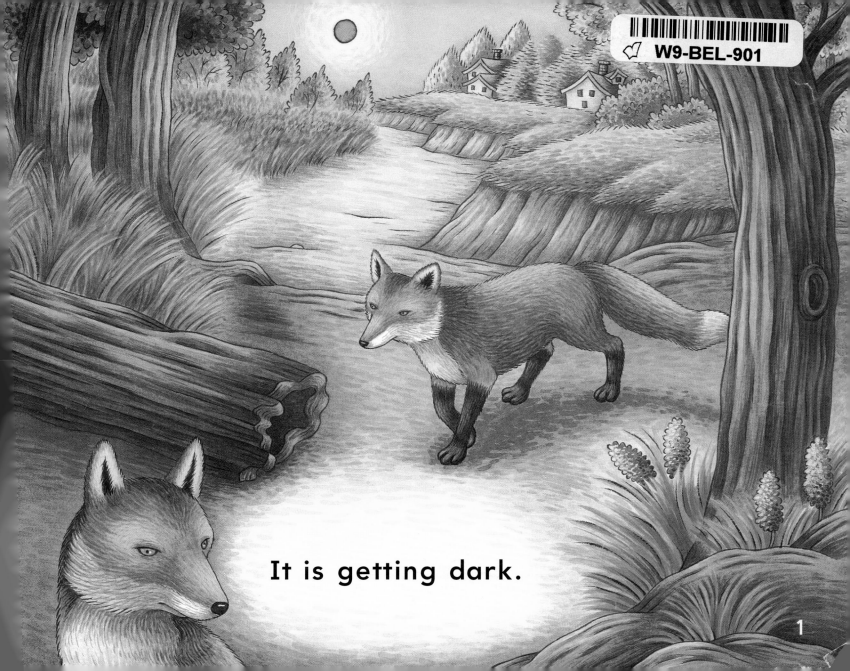

It is getting dark.

A red fox sits by her den.

She has six baby foxes.
They are very little.

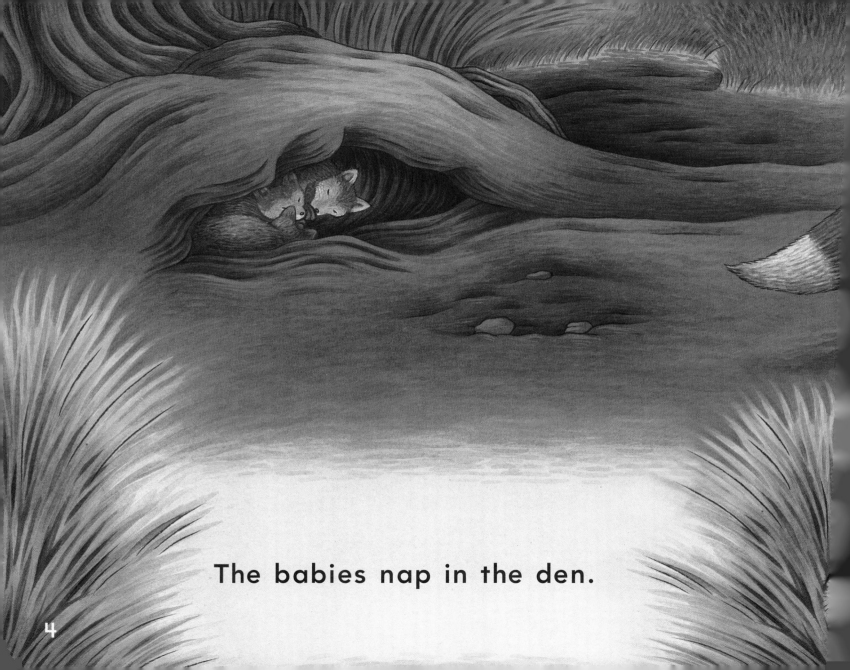

The babies nap in the den.

The mother fox goes out to find food.

Now it is morning.
The baby foxes get up.

The mother fox is back with food
for her babies.

These baby foxes are well fed!